24-

D1241573

Wizards

Monsters
and Mythical Creatures

Wizards

Gail B. Stewart

ReferencePoint
Press®

San Diego, CA

APR 0 8 2013

© 2013 ReferencePoint Press, Inc.
Printed in the United States

For more information, contact:
ReferencePoint Press, Inc.
PO Box 27779
San Diego, CA 92198
www.ReferencePointPress.com

LIBRARY OF CONGRESS CATALOGING-IN-PUBLICATION DATA

Stewart, Gail B. (Gail Barbara), 1949-
Wizards / by Gail B. Stewart.
   p. cm. -- (Monsters and mythical creatures)
Includes bibliographical references and index.
ISBN 978-1-60152-470-6 (hardback) -- ISBN 1-60152-470-6 (hardback)
1. Magic. 2. Wizards. I. Title.
BF1611.S798 2013
133.4'3--dc23
                                                                            2012020755

Contents

Dangerous Magic

Three friends—Kalfur, Halfdan, and Saemunder—yearn to become wizards. According to an Icelandic folktale, the boys decide to make the long journey to the Black School, a famed academy that teaches all the skills necessary to perform magic, cast spells, and concoct potions. Upon arrival the boys find that the school is a bleak and dreary place, most of it underground within a maze of narrow tunnels.

A Strange School

Even so, they are anxious to be admitted. After knocking on the door, they are greeted by the headmaster—a menacing, unsmiling man who agrees to teach them everything they need to know to become powerful wizards. However, he explains, after the five to seven years of intense study required, one pupil—usually chosen because he is the last one ready to walk out the door—must remain at the Black School forever. The three boys accept the bargain, secretly thinking that by the time they have been at the school for that long, they will certainly have learned enough magic to escape this fate when the time comes.

As the months go by the boys adjust to the strange life at the Black School. Because there are no windows, the pupils cannot see the sky or anything else

> ## Did You Know?
> The Harry Potter books have been translated into seventy different languages.

that might distract them from their studies. There are no teachers, but the magical textbooks, with their blazing, fiery letters, keep the students at their tasks. The boys do not even see the cooks who prepare and serve their food. According to one version of the legend, "a shaggy grey hand came through the wall every day with the pupils' meals, and when they had finished eating and drinking took back the [cups] and platters."[1]

But though the atmosphere is dreary, the three friends find their studies fascinating, and they learn rapidly. The days and years go by, and eventually it is almost time for them to leave—to climb the steep stairway to the East Door that will allow them to reenter the outer world. Of course, although they are all eager to depart, no one wants to be the last to do so and thereby be singled out by the headmaster to remain forever.

Wizards with extraordinary powers have populated legends and folklore but are equally visible in contemporary literature and film. Gandalf, a wizard of great power and wisdom, is pictured in a scene from the 2001 movie The Lord of the Rings: The Fellowship of the Ring.

A Wise Plan

The morning the boys are scheduled to leave the school, Saemunder whispers to Kalfur and Halfdan that they should go out the door first. Though the two are relieved that they will not be last, they are worried about what will become of their friend. But Saemunder, the cleverest of the three boys, has come up with a plan.

He has studied hard, paying special attention to the astronomy charts that enable a wizard to know precisely the movements of the sun and moon each day. As the moment approaches when the East Door will open to release them to the outside world, Saemunder dons a wizard's robe that is several sizes too large for him and takes his place at the end of the line. The moment the door opens, everyone scrambles to escape.

The headmaster tries to seize Saemunder but is left holding only a handful of the robe Saemunder has slipped out from under. The boy is almost out the door when the headmaster points his wand at him. But right at that instant—just as Saemunder has calculated it—the sun rises, and the blazing light coming through the East Door momentarily blinds the old wizard. Unable to see Saemunder, the furious headmaster is powerless to stop him, and the boy goes free. The door slams shut, and a jubilant Saemunder rushes to catch up to his friends.

According to one retelling of the tale, "They made a curious sight as they walked into the East, if anyone had been on that lonely plain to see them. For although there were three of them, only two of them were followed by a shadow."[2] Though the headmaster had been unable to stop Saemunder from escaping, he had managed to capture the boy's shadow, which Saemunder never regains. This does not appear to limit him in any way, however, because he becomes forever known as a very great wizard who outwitted one of the most powerful wizards who ever lived.

A World Full of Wizards

Wizards have been a part of legends and folklore since primitive times. Stories involving wizards are some of the most exciting, and often the most frightening, of the world's legends from ages past. In tales originating from Siberia to Ecuador, from England to Nigeria, wizards share one thing in common—a mysterious ability to control the world around them with magical powers.

But the subject of wizards is not limited to stories from centuries ago. J.R.R. Tolkien's *Lord of the Rings* trilogy is a popular twentieth-century saga of a strange world that features a powerful wizard named Gandalf. More recently, the Harry Potter books by J.K. Rowling have introduced wizardry to millions of readers around the world. Wizards also appear as popular characters in perennial favorite movies such as *The Princess Bride, The Wizard of Oz,* and the Star Wars films. They also figure prominently in a range of video and role-playing games and occasionally even in musical compositions.

Given the wide range of venues in which wizards continue to appear, it is obvious that the interest in these beings and the spells they create are as fascinating in the twenty-first century as they were many centuries ago.

Chapter 1

Wizards of Wisdom in Literature and Lore

One reason wizards have been such a staple in folklore and literature for generations is that magic itself seemed so vital to the earliest humans. Their lives were filled with danger; whether the threat was disease, a scarcity of food, storms, or attacks by wild animals, early human tribes had much to fear.

Necessary Magic

To protect themselves, these tribes looked for ways to appease the spirits that they believed inhabited the natural world around them—the trees, mountains, rivers, and sky. Notes folklore expert Robert Curran:

> These spirits were not always helpful to humans, but some humans found they might be pleaded with, tricked, or bribed into kindness. It eventually occurred to our early ancestors to ask, "What if we could use the forces that lie in the natural world to make life better for ourselves?" And so the first concept of magic was born.[3]

Among early societies, a few people demonstrated an ability to communicate with the spirit world. These were the first wizards, and others consulted them about matters such as the best time to plant crops or the locations where hunters would have the most success in finding game. These early wizards learned to use plants and spells that helped heal the wounded and sick. They used secret words and incantations to predict the future and placate the spirits to ensure the community's safety and prosperity.

Eventually, according to folklore and legend, wizards grew even more successful, and their communities held them in the greatest esteem. Called wise ones, sorcerers, enchanters, shamans, and diviners, among other names, these magic makers perfected casting spells, creating potions, and carrying out a wide range of other magical actions. And the magic these wise wizards performed has been a source of delight and suspense in stories and legends.

Shape-Shifting

One of the most fantastic abilities of a wizard is that of shape-shifting—changing from human to animal and sometimes even to a nonliving thing such as a rock or a strong wind. In one well-known African legend, a young wizard named Auta is eager to try this magic—and have a little fun in the process.

> ## Did You Know?
>
> Some legendary wizards consult a leather-bound book of spells known as a *grimoire*.

As his nonmagical brothers are playing draughts (a game much like checkers), Auta changes himself into a sleek black stallion. For fun, he instructs his brothers to put a bridle on him, take him to the city, and sell him. They do as he asks, selling him to a king for a great price—eight elephants. After the king rides him to his palace, Auta suddenly bolts and runs away. Furious that he has lost his beautiful new horse, the king orders his own wizard to change into a horse himself to bring the new stallion back.

What follows is a high-speed, shape-shifting battle. As the king's wizard-horse pursues him, the Auta-horse changes into a white eagle. The other wizard becomes a black eagle and gives chase. Auta becomes a hawk, and the king's wizard becomes a falcon. As the two birds soar over Auta's brothers, who are still at their game, Auta changes into a draught and clatters onto the game board.

The king's wizard changes back into a man and demands the brothers hand over the draught piece. They are surprised by the man's appearance, but after counting the pieces on the board, they agree that they have one piece too many. The brothers are about to hand over the draught when it changes into a scorpion a split second before it falls into the wizard's outstretched hand. As Auta's brothers look on in awe, the shape-shifting continues; the wizard becomes a striped snake to eat the scorpion, and the scorpion instantly becomes a larger speckled snake.

Eventually Auta suggests to the king's wizard that they return to their human forms. The king's wizard is impressed with Auta's skill, and Auta is pleased to have been able to compete with such an accomplished wizard. The folktale ends with the king's wizard returning to the king, whose disappointment at losing his horse is lessened by the return of the eight elephants, which have since wandered back to the palace.

Potions

In addition to shape-shifting, another trait shared by benevolent wizards is the knowledge of creating potions. By mixing a concoction of natural substances—almost always in very specific amounts and in a carefully regimented order—wizards have been able to create potions that can cure even the most acute illnesses and injuries.

J.K. Rowling frequently describes the potion-making ability of wizards in her Harry Potter books. For example, in *Harry Potter and the Chamber of Secrets*, Harry and his friends Ron and Hermione want to find out whether Harry's enemy Draco Malfoy and his pals Crabbe and Goyle are involved with some dangerous doings at Hogwarts, the boarding school they all attend. Searching in the restricted section of the school's library, Hermione discovers a recipe for something called Polyjuice Potion, which enables a person to as-

sume the appearance of another. Hermione hopes that by drinking the potion Harry and Ron can take on the appearance of Crabbe and Goyle and find out what they are plottting.

Polyjuice Potion contains many exotic ingredients, including twelve lacewing flies that have been stewed for twenty-one days, four leeches with their suckers removed, the dried skin of a poison-ous snake called a boomslang, as well as a bit—usually a hair—from the person one wants to turn into. Hermione gathers the ingredients and mixes them, and the friends wait a month for the potion to brew. The potion works as planned, although Rowling describes Harry's transformation into Gregory Goyle, a much bigger boy, as quite an unpleasant experience:

> Immediately, his insides started writhing as though he'd just swallowed live snakes—doubled up, he wondered whether he was going to be sick—then a burning sensation spread rapidly from his stomach to the very ends of his fingers and toes—next, bringing him gasping to all fours, came to a horrible melting feeling, as the skin all over his body bubbled like hot wax—and before their eyes, his hands began to grow, the fingers thickened, the knuckles were bulging like bolts—his shoulders stretched painfully and a prickling on his forehead told him that his hair was creeping down toward his eyebrows—his robes ripped as his chest expanded like a barrel bursting its hoops—his feet were agony in shoes four sizes too small.[4]

The Wizard's Shop

In some stories wizard potions produce effects much more pleasant than those of Polyjuice Potion. In a short story published in 1901 called "The Magic Bonbons," L. Frank Baum—the creator of *The Wizard of Oz*—tells of a Boston wizard named Dr. Daws, whose shop specializes in magical potions that are delicious as well as effective. A young woman, Claribel, comes into the shop and explains that she wants to become a world-famous entertainer, but unfortunately she cannot sing, dance, act, play an instrument, perform acrobatics, or even speak confidently in front of other people. Can Dr. Daws provide her with some potion that will help?

The wizard, who practices what he calls "chemical sorcery,"[5] instructs her to return the following day, and he will have prepared something that will enable her to achieve her goal. When Claribel comes back, he presents her with a small box of what look like

The Cat Did It

In *Scandinavian Folk Belief and Legend*, editors Reimund Kvideland and Henning K. Sehmsdorf include a story told by a Danish woman in 1932 about a local wizard who was able to find a food thief in a strange way:

"Once, my uncle, bookbinder Wiwel from Frederiksborg, was talking to the owner of an inn in town. They were saying how odd it was that the fish they had planned to eat for dinner had disappeared from the kitchen. Somebody must have stolen it because they had seen it a little earlier.

An old beggar happened to be at the inn, sitting by himself. People said that he could strike out a thief's eye. When they asked him, he did not deny it, and promised to strike out the eye of whoever had stolen the fish.

With a piece of chalk, he drew a circle on the table and surrounded it with some scrawls. Then he took a hammer and nail and muttered something while he fixed the nail at the center of the circle.

'Now it is done,' he said.

They sat and waited. Suddenly the black family cat came running. One of her eyes was all bloody and torn. There had not been anything wrong with the cat before, so they knew that the cat had been the thief."

Quoted in Reimund Kvideland and Henning K. Sehmsdorf, eds., *Scandinavian Folk Belief and Legend*. Minneapolis: University of Minnesota Press, 1988, p. 149.

beautiful French bonbons, each a different pastel color. Dr. Daws explains that each of the candies has a different purpose:

> If you eat this one with the lavender color you can dance thereafter as lightly and gracefully as if you had been trained a lifetime. After you consume the pink . . . you will sing like a nightingale. Eating the white one will enable you to become the finest [public speaker] in the land. The chocolate piece will charm you into playing the piano better than [twelve-year-old prodigy Arthur] Rubenstein, while after eating your lemon-yellow bonbon you can easily kick six feet above your head.[6]

Excited at the possibilities before her, Claribel writes Dr. Daws a generous check and leaves the shop. Stopping to do another errand, however, she accidentally leaves the box behind and a little girl named Bessie Bostwick picks it up with her own parcels. Bessie does not even notice she has the candy until she arrives home. The candy looks delicious, and she sets it out on a table after helping herself to the chocolate one.

The Mix-Up

Instantly Bessie is seized by an impulse to play the piano. Her parents stare in disbelief at their daughter, who is suddenly playing piano pieces usually attempted only by professionals. When the Bostwicks' dinner guests—a senator and a professor—arrive, they too are amazed at the girl's ability.

Mr. Bostwick pops the pink bonbon into his mouth and offers the other candies to his guests. The professor eats the lemon-yellow piece, and the senator chooses the lavender one and decides to save it for later. Mrs. Bostwick takes the white bonbon. Chaos immediately ensues: Bessie's father begins singing in a loud, startling soprano voice, and the professor kicks so high that the chandelier is in danger. Mrs. Bostwick begins reciting the poem "The Charge of the Light Brigade," though no one pays any attention to her. Bessie continues to play one song after the other, oblivious to her surroundings. Horrified by the insanity around him, the senator departs.

The following day the senator is scheduled to speak at an important political meeting. Just before he is introduced he remembers the lavender bonbon in his coat pocket, and he slips it into his mouth to clear his throat. Within a minute or two he begins speaking, but he is soon seized by the impulse to dance. Leaping and pointing his toes as well as the most highly trained ballet dancer, he thoroughly embarrasses his supporters and friends.

The story ends with the explanation that Claribel, the original owner of the bonbons, went back to Dr. Daws to purchase another box of the candies. "She must have taken better care of these," Baum writes, "for she is now a famous vaudeville actress."[7]

> **Did You Know?**
>
> Shamans of Native American communities were often called medicine men by white settlers.

Helping Sailors Find Their Way

The ability to create potions, although helpful, is not a necessity for wizards. Some wizards have other magical talents that prove even more valuable. Legends of John Dimond, who was known as a wizard in his eighteenth-century Marblehead, Massachusetts, community, describe his ability to guide ships to safety during dangerous storms. When the weather threatened, Dimond went to the old cemetery outside of town. From there he was somehow able to direct ships safely to port—even though he was miles away from them. Folklorist Charles M. Skinner, in his 1896 book *Myths and Legends of Our Own Land*, explains:

Vessels were trying to enter the port of Marblehead in a heavy gale or at night, their crews were startled to hear a trumpet voice pealing from the skies, plainly audible above the howling and hissing of any tempest, telling them how to lay their course so as to reach smooth water. This was the voice of Dimond, speaking from his station, miles away in the village cemetery. He always repaired to this place in troublous weather and shouted orders to the ships that were made visible to him by mystic power as he strode to and fro among the graves.[8]

In one eighteenth-century legend, a benevolent wizard guides ships to safety during dangerous storms off the coast of Massachusetts. Such storms represented a real threat to ships unfortunate enough to be caught in them, as suggested by the 1803 painting America of Marblehead.

Most puzzling was how Dimond knew the names of the captains and ships he was addressing, notes Robert Curran:

He would call out ... things like "Captain Jasper McClelland of the *Elizabeth Anne,* do you hear me? Steer four degrees to starboard and run true until you reach the Halfway Rock," or, "Captain Benjamin Rowe of the *Hetty,* hear my words. Move six degrees to port or you will founder on a hidden shoal." ... Some [of the names] were known to him and some were not, but he got every captain and vessel correct.[9]

Testing

Although many legends, including those of John Dimond, feature wizards who are helpful to humans, others depict wizards who desire to test a person's character. Such wizards often disguise themselves and devise a situation in which a person's character is revealed either to be petty and greedy or generous and kind. The wizard usually punishes the former and richly rewards the latter.

One such story is an old Hungarian tale called "The Silver Penny." A soldier named Marzi returns home from a war and is saddened to learn that his father has recently died. Marzi's brothers and sisters have divided up the father's wealth, leaving Marzi only a silver penny. Disappointed, but accepting his lot, Marzi pockets the coin and goes on his way.

Soon he meets an old beggar who asks for anything Marzi can spare. The kindhearted Marzi gives the beggar the only thing in his own pocket, the silver penny. The beggar then reveals himself to be a wizard, wearing a cloak made of oak leaves (oak trees were often sacred to wizards). The wizard praises Marzi for his generosity and offers to grant the young man any wish he desires. After thinking a moment, Marzi replies that he wants to experience what it would be like to be a dove, a salmon, and a hare. The wizard grants him the wish, and the two part company.

Not long afterward Marzi crosses the border into another country and is asked to join its army. The king possesses a magic ring, and as long as he wears it, his army will not be defeated. But one day, as the king and his army struggle against a stronger enemy, the king realizes that he has left his ring at home. He announces, "The man that fetches me my ring before they are overpowered by the enemy shall have the hand of my only daughter as his reward."[10]

Fetching the Ring

But the ride from the battlefield to the palace is a long one, requiring at least seven days and seven nights; thus, no one offers to try to fetch the ring. Marzi, however, in possession of his magic gifts, quickly volunteers. Announcing that he will hold the king to his promise, Marzi assumes the form of a hare and speeds away, leaving the soldiers awestruck. When he comes to a wide river, he changes into a salmon to

Gandalf the Wizard

Gandalf was a great wizard in J.R.R. Tolkien's *The Hobbit* and *The Lord of the Rings*. The stories take place in a mythical location called Middle-earth about six thousand years ago. Gandalf first appears as Gandalf the Grey, an old man with kind eyes, a long gray beard, a pointed hat, and a long coat who uses limited magical skills to fight evil forces. He carries a staff to cast spells, light a path to help an escape, or repel his foes. With his sword he can cause a lightning strike. In other times of trouble he talks to a moth to summon a great eagle he had once helped. His horse, Shadowfax, can be ridden without a bridle; Gandalf directs him with his mind.

During his two thousand years in Middle-earth, the wizard sympathizes with the weak. He uses his wisdom and reputation to guide the elves and dwarves, and he creates fear to ward off evil forces. Gandalf dies in battle, but during the fight he is able to collapse a bridge with his staff, causing the death of his opponent. Later his spirit comes back in another human body as Gandalf the White, the most powerful wizard of all. He is so powerful that he can temporarily blind an opponent with a flash of light or send him flying into the air merely by slamming his staff to the ground.

swim across it, and afterward changes into a dove to soar over the trees. In a fraction of the time it would have taken him without the wizard's gifts, he arrives at the palace and introduces himself to the princess. She gives Marzi her father's ring and sends him on his way.

But one of the other soldiers almost ruins everything. Having seen Marzi change into a hare, he decides to hide behind a tree, waiting until the hare returns with the ring in its mouth. The soldier shoots the hare with an arrow, killing it. He proudly presents the ring to the overjoyed king, who proclaims that the soldier will be wed to the princess.

In the meantime, however, the wizard has been keeping watch over Marzi. He witnesses the soldier killing the hare, and recognizing that the hare is really Marzi, he casts a spell that brings him back to life. He urges Marzi to rush to the palace to prevent the devious soldier from marrying the princess. When Marzi arrives, the princess is overjoyed. The king punishes the false bridegroom, wins the battle against the enemy army, and proclaims Marzi king of the lands he has just conquered.

The Most Famous Wizard of All

Although the talents of many wizards in folklore and literature are impressive, none surpasses those of Merlin (in some texts spelled Merlyn), the wizard who is credited with helping the legendary King Arthur come to power in England. The first person believed to have written about Merlin was Geoffrey of Monmouth, the twelfth-century author of *History of the Kings of Britain*.

According to Geoffrey, Merlin was an adviser to a series of kings, beginning in the fifth century with Vortigern, followed by Ambrose, and then Uther, who was said to be Arthur's father. Merlin, like many other legendary wizards, is only half human. His mother was a Welsh princess, and his father a mysterious demon—a heritage that was believed to account for his magical abilities.

One of the first examples of Merlin's magic occurs when he is just a boy. In the story he is brought before King Vortigern, who has been trying to build a tall lookout tower on a hill in what is now Wales. However, every night all the progress his workers make during the day is mysteriously undone, and the tower collapses. To solve the problem, the king's priests tell him that he needs to sacrifice a fatherless boy and sprinkle the boy's blood in the foundation of the tower. They promise that once that is done, the tower will stand.

Young Merlin has no father, so he is a likely candidate to shed his blood for the king's tower. When brought to the building site,

> # Did You Know?
> Some legends say that the tree in which Merlin was entrapped by Vivien (or Nimue) is in Broceliande, a wooded area in Brittany in northwest France.

however, Merlin tells the king that deep underneath the building site is a lake, and at the bottom of the lake is a stone chest containing two dragons—one white and the other red. Every night the dragons fight one another, which causes the tower to fall.

The king's priests are skeptical that the boy can know things that they themselves do not. But Vortigern orders his workers to dig down under the foundation. To their astonishment, they discover a lake, just as Merlin described. Exploring further, they find the stone chest and the dragons, too. Merlin explains that the red dragon represents Vortigern and his people, and the white dragon represents the invading Saxons. As the fighting dragons become visible to the onlookers, the red dragon defeats the white one, though it dies in the battle. It is a sobering prediction for the king and his realm, but Merlin has established himself as a wizard whom future kings will consult on weighty matters.

Mentoring Wart

Another important use of Merlin's legendary magic is in educating young Arthur—known by the nickname "Wart" in T.H. White's retelling of the legend. Merlin, foreseeing that Wart will become king, uses a great deal of magic to teach Wart important lessons that will enable him as ruler to be not only mighty and powerful but also fair, thoughtful, and wise. Merlin's magic allows Wart to experience life in a number of forms—including those of fish, ants, snow geese, and badgers—and in a number of societies.

For his first such adventure, Merlin changes Wart into a perch living in the castle's moat and disguises himself as a carp. Wart comes face to face with a huge pike, the sharp-toothed king of the moat, who tells Wart that the only important thing in fish life is total power. "Power of the body decides everything in the end," the pike tells him, "and only Might is Right."[11] Then he lunges at Wart to try to kill him. Wart barely gets away in time, and Merlin changes him back into a boy.

Transformed later into an ant, Wart works in a dreary, violent colony, doing menial labor whose value he does not understand. There is no pleasure in a job completed, nor is there a feeling of community when the ants are working. Instead, there is only the fear of being idle. Wart realizes that the limits of such a situation extend even to language. "There were no words for happiness, for freedom, for liking, nor were there any words for their opposites," White writes. "The nearest [Wart] could get to Right or Wrong, even, was to say Done or Not Done."[12]

Merlin, the most famous wizard of all time, plays a central role in stories of King Arthur—both ancient and modern. In these stories Merlin displays an extraordinary range of magical abilities.

As a result of Merlin's magic, Wart is well prepared to become a wise leader. He has learned that as king, he must not rely on fear and aggression for control, like the pike, and that he must value his subjects' individuality rather than forcing them to be mindless servants like the worker ants.

The Undoing of Merlin

Although wizards like Merlin may have a dizzying array of magical abilities, they are not infallible, nor are they immortal. According to folklore, Merlin becomes occasionally foolish as he grows older, especially around beautiful young women. This proves to be his undoing.

One breathtakingly beautiful woman named Vivien (or in some versions of the legend, Nimue) is determined to learn Merlin's magic. Normally a wizard would never think of revealing his secrets, but Vivien uses her beauty and flattery to convince Merlin to tell her how he performs some of his most powerful spells.

Once she has coaxed that information from him, Vivien makes Merlin helpless by changing him into an oak tree.

The circumstances of Merlin's end vary in legend. According to some versions of the story, Merlin died, his soul imprisoned within the tree. Others say that he remains within the oak tree in a state of suspended animation, waiting to return until Britain needs him again someday. Merlin, like many benevolent wizards in folklore, is beloved for standing against the dark forces that have so often threatened and frightened human beings.

Chapter 2

Wizards and the Dark Arts

Although some wizards of legend are benevolent and willing to help people, a great many are not. These wizards often use their powers for their own selfish gains. It is not uncommon for them to harm or even kill people who anger them or get in their way. The magic these wizards are said to practice is often referred to as "the Dark Arts."

The Sorceress Circe

Though most wizards in folklore and literature are male, a few are women—often called sorceresses. One of the most famous is Circe, who appears in the epic poem *The Odyssey*, written in the eighth century BC by the poet Homer. The poem tells the story of a Greek warrior named Odysseus who is attempting to return home after the ten-year-long Trojan War. Odysseus and his men encounter many dangerous obstacles on the journey; at one point, hopelessly lost, they land on an unfamiliar island.

Odysseus's second in charge, Eurylochus, takes half of the crew to explore the island and see whether someone there can help them get back on course. After a while Eurylochus and the men arrive at a stone house—the sorceress Circe's house—in the middle of the forest. Though they do not yet know who lives there, they realize right away that something is very wrong, as Odysseus later recalls:

There were wild mountain wolves and lions prowling all round it—poor bewitched creatures whom she had tamed by her enchantments and drugged into subjection. They did not attack my men, but wagged their great tails, fawned upon them, and rubbed their noses lovingly against them. As hounds crowd round their master when they see him coming from dinner—for they know he will bring them something—even so did these wolves and lions with their great claws fawn upon my men, but the men were terribly frightened at seeing such strange creatures.[13]

Turning Men into Pigs

The men then go to the front door, where Circe meets them. She invites them in, but Eurylochus stays behind, watching. The sorceress prepares the men a bracing drink, lacing it with one of her potions, which has a horrifying effect on them. As Odysseus explains:

When they had drunk she turned them into pigs by a stroke of her wand, and shut them up in her pigsties. They were like pigs—head, hair, and all, and they grunted just as pigs do; but their senses were the same as before, and they remembered everything. Thus then were they shut up squealing, and Circe threw them some acorns and beech masts such as pigs eat.[14]

Eurylochus hurries back to the camp to explain what has happened. With a heavy heart, Odysseus sets off for Circe's house. On the way he meets the god Hermes, who gives him a special herb called moly that will make him immune to Circe's potions.

The moly works as Hermes promises; although Odysseus drinks the same poisoned drink his men were served, it does not affect him. Drawing his sword, Odysseus threatens to kill Circe if she does not return his men to their human forms. However, Circe proposes a trade: She will change them back if he promises to stay with her for a year. Though Odysseus has a wife back in Greece, he knows he must agree to Circe's terms to save his men.

In the epic poem The Odyssey *the sorceress Circe turns Odysseus's men into pigs. Odysseus manages to overcome her dark magic with a potion from the god Hermes and a promise to stay with Circe for a year.*

The Finmen

Although the stories of Odysseus originated in ancient Greece, the Orkney Islands of northern Scotland have legends about a race of hooded wizards called Finmen, who also can be extremely dangerous to humans. Finmen are amphibious, able to survive on land and underwater. They are said to spend the long winters in

Finfolkaheem, their beautiful underwater city. Finfolkaheem, according to many Orkney storytellers, is a true wizard paradise:

> Lit by the phosphorescent glow of the sea, Finfolkaheem was decorated with swathes of draped curtains whose colours shifted like the ever-changing shades of the "Merry Dancers"—the Aurora Borealis. Towers of glistening white coral spiraled upwards, encrusted with pearls and precious gemstones. . . . Like the true gentry of their underwater world, they herded whales—from which they extracted milk—and, mounted on their aquatic steeds, would often hunt the animals of the sea using otters in place of dogs.[15]

Not surprisingly, the Finmen are superb fishermen and expert sailors. Using magic, a Finman can cross from Orkney to Norway or Iceland in an astonishing seven strokes of his oar. Finmen dislike and distrust humans, especially fishermen, because the Finmen consider them trespassers on their fishing grounds.

The Aggression of the Finmen

Sometimes Finmen try to avoid curious humans completely by surrounding their own boats with a thick mist or by simply making themselves invisible. They also have many ways of discouraging fishermen from straying too close to their domain. One is to use magic to drive fish away from coastal areas, where humans typically fish.

Finmen also have a more aggressive method of dealing with fishermen: they simply seize the human's line and hang on until it breaks. If that does not drive a fisherman from the area, the Finmen damage the human's boat during the night by tearing a hole in the bottom or smashing the oars. Sometimes the Finmen actually kidnap a human they feel is a threat to them. They take him down to their underwater kingdom, where he will eventually marry one of the Finwomen. Scottish fishermen who heard these stories were terrified of run-ins with the Finmen.

Did You Know?

Finmen were said to value silver above anything and would never part with a silver coin.

The Dangers of the Finmen

In one often-repeated Orkney tale, a boatman was once hired by a hooded stranger to take him and a cow over to a distant island. Even though it would be a long, difficult trip, the boatman agreed to the job because the stranger promised him more than twice his regular fee. Part of the way through the journey, however, the boatman realized with a shock that the hooded, silent stranger was a Finman, a sorcerer of the Orkneys. Keeping his fear in check, the boatman took the Finman and his cow to the island and returned home—relieved that he lived to tell the tale.

A year afterward, the boatman spotted the same Finman at an unlikely place—a busy fair. Being a friendly man, the boatman greeted him politely, said that it was good to see him, and offered to buy the Finman a drink. Furious that a mortal would dare to speak to him in a familiar way, as well as angry that the boatman had recognized him, the Finman reached into the folds of his cloak. According to one version of the story, "[He] pulled out a box with powder in it and blew some into the boatman's eyes. From that moment on, the boatman was blinded and remained so for the remainder of his life."

Sigurd Towrie, "A Close Tongue Keeps a Safe Head," Orkneyjar. www.orkneyjar.com.

Necromancy

Though wizards like the Finmen are wicked by nature, many others are guilty merely of careless dabbling in the Dark Arts. For example, stories abound of those who have practiced a type of magic called necromancy. This is a practice used to make contact with the dead to predict the future or to gain information not readily available in other ways. Using necromancy, wizards are said to be capable of raising the dead or at least summoning their spirits.

The Catholic Church considered such magic sinful and officially condemned it during the fifth century. Church leaders pointed to the Old Testament of the Bible, which is very clear on the subject: "There shall not be found among you [any one] that . . . uses divination, [or] an observer of times, or an enchanter, or a witch, or a charmer, or a consulter with familiar spirits, or a wizard, or a necromancer. For all that do these things [are] an abomination unto the Lord."[16]

Even though the intent of a wizard using necromancy was not necessarily to harm anyone, the practice was still thoroughly condemned. Magicians who practiced necromancy were often jailed, excommunicated from the Catholic Church, or even executed. In 1600 Italian friar Giordano Bruno was found guilty of heresy for, among other things, simply writing a treatise defending such magic. Bruno was sentenced to burn at the stake.

Disposing of a Necromancer's Book

Books pertaining to necromancy were believed to be actual magical objects, not simply instructions for those who wanted to perform such magic. Historian Richard Kieckhefer provides an account of how a book on magic could not only provide direction on how to perform magic but also possess magical properties. Kieckhefer tells the story of Antonius, a fifteenth-century archbishop in Florence, Italy, who went to have his hair cut one day. The barber, like most barbers in those times, was also a surgeon. The archbishop asked him how he could cure people without knowing Latin, the language of educated people. The barber explained that he had received a special book that taught him everything he needed to know. When he showed it to Antonius, the archbishop was horrified to see that

Wizards who attempted to raise the dead, known as necromancers, were often condemned as practitioners of the dark arts. The Art of Necromancy, *artwork from the thirteenth century, depicts the work of the necromancer.*

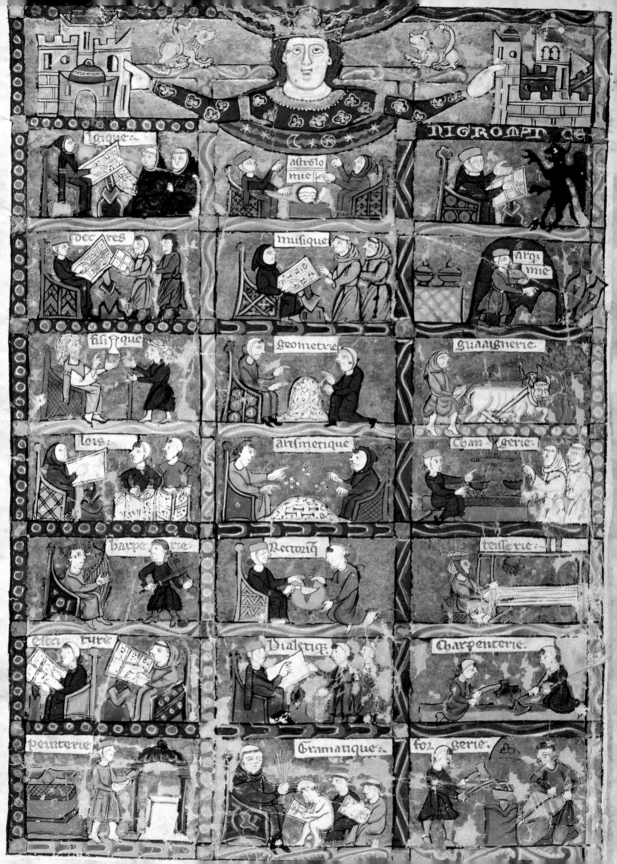

it contained many incantations and symbols used in the Dark Arts. The archbishop confiscated the book and soon afterward decided to dispose of it—with frightening consequences:

> He had fire brought in an earthen vessel, and he set fire to the book. Immediately the air was so darkened that the citizens were afraid, and clung to the archbishop. He comforted them, saying that when the book was fully burned this darkening and clouding of the air would cease, as indeed happened. . . . Wherever the book was, a multitude of demons resided there.[17]

Scrying

Despite the disapproval of society and the Catholic Church, throughout the centuries magicians have continued to practice necromancy. One of the most common means of contacting the spirit world is a method called scrying. This process involves summoning aid from a spirit residing within an object with a smooth surface—a crystal ball, a bowl of water that is sometimes colored with ink, a mirror, the shiny blade of a knife or sword, or even the smooth face of a gemstone.

"Though people don't always recognize the term 'scrying,' almost everyone—even the smallest children—can recall seeing it in books and films," says La Vol, a Belgian-born fortune-teller who has dabbled in scrying for more than twelve years. "Think of a fortune teller with a crystal ball. Or think of the Queen in the story of Snow White. She has a mirror whose spirit can tell her the answer to every question. So she asks the spirit in the magic mirror, 'Who's the fairest one of all?' When the spirit in the mirror tells her that Snow White is, she goes quite berserk."[18]

<aside>

Did You Know?

European wizards, when casting a spell, traditionally waved their hand from left to right, since the opposite way was considered very bad luck.

</aside>

Crime Fighting by Scrying

One manuscript from the fifteenth century describes how scrying was used to solve a crime. An important landowner in Yorkshire,

England, hired a laborer who was notorious for his large appetite. The worker was staying in the lord's manor, and he frequently crept downstairs to the kitchen in the middle of the night to steal pieces of meat to eat.

When the lord noticed the dwindling supply of meat, he first questioned his servants. They all swore that they had not stolen the food, and the lord believed them. Puzzled, he contacted a wizard specializing in necromancy and directed him to solve the mystery. When the laborer heard that a wizard had been called in, he was frightened. He went to the priests in town, confessed his wrongdoing, and begged them to absolve him of the crimes.

Meanwhile, the wizard began his investigation. He summoned a young boy, under the age of twelve, to help in the ceremony. After anointing the boy's fingernail with oil, the wizard recited some magic charms and spells, then asked the boy to look at the fingernail and describe what he saw. Like many necromancers, the wizard believed that the spirit he was calling on for help might be more willing to reveal images to a child than to himself.

The Value of a Fingernail

According to the manuscript, the wizard's methods worked. Staring at his fingernail, the boy saw the image of a worker with a short haircut. "Look at that!" the boy added. "I see a really beautiful horse!"[19]

The wizard next asked the boy to describe the man in more detail. In response, the boy gave a description of the laborer walking downstairs and cutting off pieces of meat. Finally, the wizard asked the boy what the laborer was doing at that instant. "[The man and his horse] are going to the church of the friars, and the horse is waiting outside," the boy answered, "and the man is going in and kneeling and speaking with one of the friars, who is putting his hand on his head [a priestly act of officially forgiving a person making a confession]."[20]

Legends say that such a vision using a scrying object lasts no more than a minute or two. Moreover, the spirit within the object cannot provide images after a wrongdoer has made a confession and been officially forgiven by a priest. In this case, when the wizard questioned the boy further as to what his fingernail showed, the boy reported, "Both of them have just vanished from my eyes. I cannot see them any more, and I have no idea where they have gone."[21]

A Terrifying Demon

According to legends and some first-person accounts, scrying can sometimes prove incredibly risky to the magician who attempts it. Notes Scottish historian P.G. Maxwell-Stuart, "What he or she does is often fraught with danger, and far from being an attractive, rather amusing cartoon figure who waves a wand and causes immediate suspension of the laws of nature, the real magician runs risks every time he works his craft."[22]

The alleged experience of a nineteenth-century amateur necromancer named Frederick Hockley is a good example. Hockley claimed to have had a frightening experience one night as he tried to follow instructions given to him by a spirit. He had been looking into a crystal for a very long time, but without success. "Before I left off," he later wrote in an article in [a magazine] called the *Spiritualist*, "I asked the spirit of the crystal, very earnestly, when I could have a vision, for it was so very wearisome to look, and to anticipate, and then be disappointed."[23]

According to his journal, he received a message from the spirit almost the instant he uttered those words. The spirit gave him detailed instructions for speeding the process along. He was told to get a large glass bottle, about a foot deep, and fill it with pond water. After that, Hockley was to cut the middle finger of his left hand and write in blood a certain name on a strip of paper and paste it to the bottle. Finally, he was to insert his finger in the bottle so that a drop of blood from the cut would drip into the water. Hockley followed the instructions— with terrifying results. The moment a drop of his blood fell into the bottle, things happened quickly:

> ## Did You Know?
>
> Simon the Mage, an evil wizard mentioned in the Bible, tried to buy the apostle Peter's miracle-working power—but without success.

The water began to change to a thick, dirty-red liquid, and from this there formed, as the water again became clearer, a spirit more like an animal than even a distorted human figure; it had a tail as long in proportion to its size as is the tail of a mouse to the rest of the animal, and it had peculiarly shaped horns. It increased in size so to fill the entire bottle.[24]

When the head of the spirit (or whatever it was) rose above the water, Hockley figured that he could keep it contained in the bottle by pressing a heavy book on top of the opening. He soon realized he had underestimated the spirit's strength:

> I am very strong—as strong, I believe, as most men—I can lift a couple of hundredweight. . . . I tried to press the book on the neck of the bottle with all my might, but I could not move it one inch. My hands and the book in them went up as easily as I could have lifted a baby's hands. I grew desperate. I tore the [piece of paper] off the bottle. . . . The spirit all this time was gradually getting out of the bottle.[25]

A Promise to Be More Careful

Hockley threw the bottle onto the floor, shattering it and spilling its contents onto the rug. He thought for a moment that the spirit had left, but from the water it rose even larger than before. Frightened, he asked the spirit what it wanted and received a strange answer:

> He asked me to test his power by naming anything I desired, and said that if I found that he gave it to me, and if I could promise him obedience, he would do the same in all other things. I resolutely told him that I would not—that if I had known he was evil and could escape from the bottle, I would not have called him.[26]

After answering the spirit, Hockley recalled, his eyes began to burn and he felt ill. He seemed to hallucinate that there were a thousand demons in the room rather than only one. Everything went dark, but soon afterward everything was bright again. The spirit and the bloody water were gone. Hockley burned the paper from the bottle, cleaned up the glass shards, and vowed that in the future he would be far more cautious.

Francis Woolcott

Slightly less terrifying than Hockley's demon was the legendary American wizard Francis Woolcott. Early in the nineteenth century Woolcott and his band of thirteen night riders were said to have terrorized the residents of Copake, a small farming community in eastern New York State. Stories about Woolcott describe him with the perfect appearance for a fearsome wizard. He was tall and dark, with protruding teeth, although a mysterious mist obscured most of his facial features. He usually wore a hood and cloak, and his sinister laugh, writes folklorist Charles M. Skinner, "used to give his neighbors a creep along their spines."[27]

Woolcott was not a farmer, nor did he appear to have any other work, but because of his fearsome reputation he was able to demand—and receive—free supplies (known as levies) of pork, cider, flour, and other things from the farmers in the county. In one legend, a woman named Sylvia Daniels recalls how, as a child, she was confused by her father's reaction when Woolcott came to her family's farm one day:

> One levy day, when I was four, I ... watched my father handing a cloaked figure a side of beef. It looked like a normal business transaction, the kind of thing my father did every day, except there was none of the joking that usually accompanied such a transaction. My father's face was grim and his eyes were full of fear. The cloaked figure of the night rider made me shiver, though it was the height of summer.[28]

The Dangers of Refusal

To refuse to pay Woolcott's levy, or to anger him in any other way, was to invite trouble. One farmer who resisted the wizard was

Horses Come to Life

In the story "The Night Riders," a young woman reminisces about the time she first witnessed the summoning of the sleek black horses used by wizard Francis Woolcott and his men:

> "I was awakened just after midnight one evening, two months after my arrival [as housekeeper for Francis Woolcott and his night riders], by the quiet sound of many feet walking down the stairs and exiting the house. I threw a dark cloak over my nightclothes and followed the night riders and Francis Woolcott out to the stables, which I saw with astonishment were empty of the proud dark horses the night riders rode. Each of the night riders entered the empty stable and came out carrying a bundle of oat straw. They carried their bundles into the center of a grove of ash and chestnut trees and placed them in a circle around the wizard. It was the dark of the moon, and the only light came from the tip of the wizard's staff as he raised it over the bundles of straw, chanting in a language that sounded foul to my ears. Before my eyes the bundles of straw transformed into thirteen dark horses that could run like the wind but could not cross moving water, and fell apart at the stroke of midnight thirty days after their creation. . . . These horses needed neither food nor sleep and could outrun any living creature. . . . Their eyes glowed red in the dark grove, and I huddled behind an ash tree and prayed the wizard would not see me."

S.E. Schlosser, *Spooky New York: Tales of Hauntings, Strange Happenings, and Other Local Lore.* Guilford, CT: Insiders' Guide, p. 124.

shocked when his cows began giving blood instead of milk. Another saw "two of our pigs strolling through the front yard, walking upright. They seemed to be discussing the weather in short snorts that sounded like words in a foreign language."[29]

The wizard did not hesitate to work his evil magic on a farmer's children as well as his animals. Writes Skinner:

> When he shouted, "Hup! Hup! Hup!" to Farmer Williams's children, had they not leaped to the moulding of the parlor wainscot—a yard above the floor and only an inch wide—and walked around it, afterward skipping like birds from chair-back to chair-back, while the furniture stood as if nailed to the floor?[30]

Old Meg

Like Woolcott, the American sorceress—or witch—Margaret Wesson was said to terrorize people in her community. Among her neighbors in Gloucester, Massachusetts, she was rumored to be an accomplished shape-shifter, often assuming the form of various birds. People also said that Old Meg, as they called her, was likely to use her magic to bring bad luck to anyone whom she disliked.

However, it was not her deeds in life for which Old Meg is most famous. In 1745 a militia group taking part in King George's War in Canada had just been victorious in battle. Two soldiers of the Massachusetts infantry were walking along, talking, when they were harassed by a large crow. No matter what they did, they could not get the crow to leave them alone. "They threw stones, and then fired their muskets at it, but could neither touch nor terrify it; the bird still continued flying round them and cawing horribly in their ears."[31]

It finally occurred to one of them that the bothersome crow might be Old Meg. Since nothing except silver was believed to have

Did You Know?

Whereas witches most often kept a cat as a familiar, or helper, wizards preferred either owls or hedgehogs.

A crystal ball might provide a glimpse into the spirit world for those who practice the art of scrying. The wizards and witches of legend sought to contact the dead through the use of crystal balls, mirrors, and even bowls of water.

any effect on black magic, the two soldiers each cut off a silver button from their uniform and rammed them into their muskets. The first bullet they shot broke the crow's leg, and the second killed it. When they finally got back to Massachusetts, they found that their suspicions about the crow's true identity had been correct. "When they returned to Gloucester, they learned that Old Meg had broken her leg while walking by the fort at the precise time when they had

shot and killed the crow five hundred miles distant," writes folklorist Samuel Adams Drake, "[and] after lingering for a while in great
agony, she died."[32]

But the most remarkable part of the legend was this: when doctors examined Old Meg's fractured leg, they found the silver buttons
the soldiers had fired into the crow. As are many good stories about
those who use the Dark Arts, this story has been repeated for many
generations—especially in Gloucester.

In most stories evil wizards do not prevail in the end. But the
chaos and fear they cause make them truly terrifying characters—and
worthy foes for those brave humans and powerful benevolent wizards
who resist them in order to keep their dark magic in check.

Chapter 3

Wizards in Popular Culture

Many centuries ago most people believed in magic and the power of wizards to harness that magic, both good and bad. Although today wizardry is not necessarily viewed the same way as it was long ago, wizards remain a fascinating subject. In fact, so-called wizards can be found in almost every segment of popular culture.

The Word *Wizard*

In modern times the much-used term *wizard* often refers to one who shows uncanny skill or ability—almost as if that person possesses some sort of magic. One well-known example is Thomas Edison, the American inventor, who in 1876 moved his science laboratory to a tiny village in New Jersey called Menlo Park.

Over the next five years Edison came up with a flurry of inventions in his new shop, from the phonograph to a telephone transmitter. Christie Street in Menlo Park was the first thoroughfare ever to be lit with incandescent light bulbs, powered by a grid Edison invented. In all, he applied for sixty-six patents during the years he spent in Menlo Park. The cover of the July 9, 1879, edition of New York's *Daily Graphic* dubbed Edison "the Wizard of Menlo Park." It featured a full-page drawing of the inventor wearing a tall, conical cap and long, flowing robes and holding a blinding flash of light in his right hand. Although Edison later moved his laboratory to New York, the nickname stuck.

Many people of Edison's time actually believed the scientist did have some almost-magical abilities—especially after a newspaper came up with an April Fools' prank about him in 1878. The publication ran a fictional account claiming that Edison had invented a "Food Creator . . . a machine that will feed the human race!"[33] It was not clear in the article how this machine worked, but supposedly it could create all kinds of delicious vegetables, wine, meat, and biscuits out of air, water, and dirt. Although the writer explained in the final paragraph that it was all a hoax, not every reader read that far. Edison received hundreds of letters from all over the United States from people marveling at his talents.

The Wizard of Baseball

The term *wizard* is often used in athletics as well as science and technology. Ozzie "the Wizard" Smith, a Hall of Fame baseball player who played with the San Diego Padres and the St. Louis Cardinals, earned his nickname for his astonishing defensive maneuvers, which seemed almost impossible for a human to accomplish. "I think of myself as an artist on the field," he says. "Every game I look for a chance to do something that the fans have never seen before."[34]

Sportswriter Ira Berkow describes Smith's near-superhuman abilities:

There was the smash under the third baseman's glove that seemed headed to left field, when Smith popped up from who knows where to backhand the ball and whip it to first. Or when he somersaulted over second base, snared the drive and spun in midair like [Soviet ballet dancer Rudolf] Nureyev to begin a double play. Or that bad hop that was about to be embedded in his forehead that he somehow barehanded before throwing out the runner at the plate.[35]

From Bullets to Wizards

The word *wizard* has also been applied to a professional basketball team—the Washington Wizards. The team's name originally was the Washington Bullets. However, owner Abe Pollin was uneasy with having the word *Bullets* in his team's name, especially in a city with one of the highest homicide rates in the nation. When his good

From Magician to Wizard

In L. Frank Baum's book *Dorothy and the Wizard in Oz*, the wizard explains that before coming to Oz, he was actually a stage magician. He had never intended to pass himself off as a real wizard, he says, but his strange name—coupled with a balloon accident—resulted in his becoming the Wizard of Oz.

"In the first place, I must tell you that I was born in Omaha, and my father, who was a politician, named me Oscar Zoroaster Phadrig Isaac Norman Henkle Emmannuel Ambroise Diggs. . . . Taken altogether, it was a dreadfully long name to weigh down a poor innocent child, and one of the hardest lessons I ever learned was to remember my own name. When I grew up I just called myself O.Z., because the other initials were P-I-N-H-E-A-D; and that spelled 'pinhead,' which was a reflection on my intelligence. . . . When a young man, I ran away from home and joined a circus, I used to call myself a Wizard, and do tricks of ventriloquism. . . . Also I began to make balloon ascensions. On my balloon and on all the other articles I used in the circus I painted the two initials: 'O.Z.', to show that those things belonged to me.

One day my balloon ran away with me and brought me down . . . to this beautiful country. When the people saw me come from the sky they naturally thought me some superior creature, and bowed down before me."

Quoted in L. Frank Baum, *Dorothy and the Wizard in Oz*. New York: Dover, 1984, pp. 192, 194.

friend Yitzhak Rabin, the Israeli prime minister, was shot by a Jewish extremist in 1995, changing the Bullets name became a personal priority for Pollin.

The Bullets invited fans to submit suggestions for the team's new name. Within six months more than two thousand ideas were proposed, including the Wizards. Although the front office never revealed the results of the fan vote, Pollin decided on the Washington Wizards. The new logo on the uniforms featured a white bearded wizard wearing a pointy hat.

Though Pollin's intention was to project a nonviolent image, with the wizard suggesting extraordinary skill in basketball, the idea backfired—because the term *wizard* is also used by the Ku Klux Klan, the white supremacist hate group that began after the Civil War and continues in a smaller form today. The title *imperial wizard* has frequently been bestowed upon the highest-ranking Klan leader.

For this reason, many in Washington, DC, found the new name as offensive as *Bullets* had been to Pollin. Explained Morris Shearin, the president of the local chapter of the National Association for the Advancement of Colored People: "When I hear [that] name I think about the Imperial Wizard or the Grand Dragon of the Ku Klux Klan."[36] In addition to the fact that the proposed logo included a wizard wearing garb resembling the hoods and cloaks of Klan members, the new name seemed a contentious choice in a city that is more than 70 percent African American.

But Pollin refused to budge. "It's someone who can do things," he said. "[A wizard] is magic, flamboyant, smart, and a winner. All those things connote a winner. Once we get the new logo and uniform and colors it'll be fantastic. The NBA [National Basketball Association] has very creative people."[37] Pollin kept the logo; however, the team was later sold and although the name Wizards continued to be used, the Wizards' logo was not.

A Humbug

Despite Pollin's view of wizards as winners, not all wizards in pop culture are competent—either as good magicians or evil ones. The wizard in L. Frank Baum's series of forty books, most notably *The Wonderful Wizard of Oz,* upon which the 1939 movie is based, is a good example. The Wizard of Oz is best known for being a phony, or humbug, for he is unable to perform any real magic at all.

During a cyclone, a young Kansas orphan named Dorothy and her dog, Toto, are transported to a magical land called Oz. Desperate to return home to her aunt and uncle who have raised her, Dorothy is told by the people of Oz that the only one who is capable of getting her back to Kansas is the Wizard of Oz.

A 1904 poster promotes a theatrical production of The Wizard of Oz. The wizard has none of the magical abilities that wizards of other tales possess. He is, in fact, a bit of a fraud as Dorothy and her friends eventually discover.

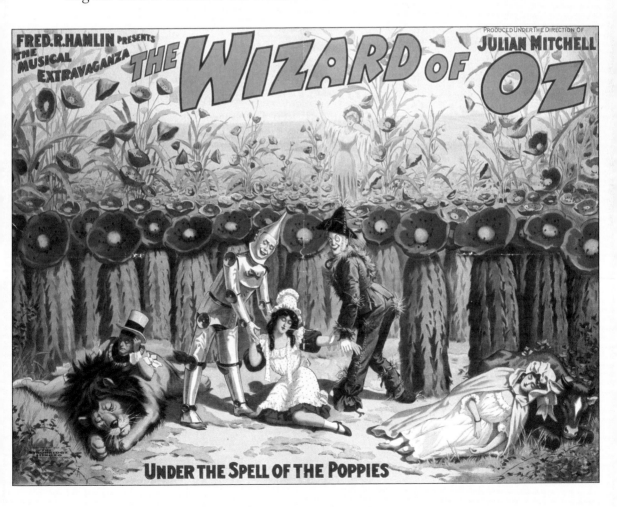

FRED. R. HANLIN PRESENTS THE MUSICAL EXTRAVAGANZA

THE WIZARD OF OZ

PRODUCED UNDER THE DIRECTION OF JULIAN MITCHELL

UNDER THE SPELL OF THE POPPIES

As she travels to the Emerald City to see the wizard, she meets three others who also are in need—a scarecrow without a brain, a tin woodman without a heart, and a fearful lion who desperately desires courage. The four eventually are granted an audience with the wizard, who appears as a giant floating green head and whose voice booms as lights flash. The wizard promises them that if they vanquish the Wicked Witch of the West, he will see to it that their requests are granted.

Although Dorothy and her friends do eventually manage to kill the Wicked Witch, the wizard turns out to be incapable of granting the four their desires. At one point, disappointed and angry that she and her friends have risked their lives against the Wicked Witch for nothing in return, Dorothy tells the wizard that he is a very bad man. He replies, "Oh no, my dear. I'm really a very good man; but I'm a very bad wizard, I must admit."[38]

The Sorcerer's Apprentice

Besides being fascinating characters in books and movies like *The Wizard of Oz*, wizards have made appearances in music as well. In fact, one of the most beloved children's movies of the twentieth century, Walt Disney's *Fantasia*, brought to life an 1897 musical composition by Paul Dukas called *The Sorcerer's Apprentice* when the film debuted in 1940.

The musical piece was inspired by an eighteenth-century poem composed by German poet Johann Wolfgang von Goethe. It tells the story of a boy who has been hired to do cleaning and other menial tasks in a wizard's castle. Sometimes the boy peeks into the room where the wizard performs his spells and watches, admiring the old man's ability.

One day, when the wizard leaves, the boy decides to put on the wizard's pointed hat and try some magic of his own. Imitating what he has seen the wizard do, the boy commands a broom

A Comic Superhero

One of the most popular of the superheroes known as Avengers, which were developed by Marvel Comics, is Sersi. Beautiful, with raven hair and lightning-fast reflexes, Sersi is, like many of the other Avengers, much older than she looks. One episode reported her to be more than five thousand years old. According to her backstory, Sersi once helped the wizard Merlin when he was threatened by a magician who practiced the Dark Arts. She has lived in ancient Rome and in France during the French Revolution, and she also once spent time with the poet Homer in ancient Greece. Sersi claims that she was the model for the sorceress Circe in Homer's famous epic poem *The Odyssey*.

In the many centuries since then, Sersi has made the decision to live in the open rather than hide her magical identity, as so many of her fellow Avengers do. She has used her fighting talents to battle the archenemies of the Avengers, known as the Deviants. Sersi, unlike most of the Avengers, enjoys living among humans. She also prides herself on her dancing and acting abilities.

to come to life and carry buckets of water so that he does not have to perform this backbreaking task himself. However, it is not long before the work is done and the boy realizes he has no idea of how to stop the broom. Taking an ax, he chops the broom in two; but then a second broom comes to life and also begins fetching water.

With the rooms soon overflowing, the boy realizes he is far out of his element. Just as it seems the castle will be destroyed by the rising tides of water, the sorcerer returns. In a single magical motion, he breaks the spell. He warns the apprentice that a sorcerer is the only one who should call on spirits to perform powerful magic.

In making *Fantasia,* Walt Disney was eager to try the then-novel technique of combining classical music with animation. The center-piece of the film was the beloved cartoon character Mickey Mouse, who starred as the sorcerer's apprentice. The groundbreaking movie cost the studio $2.25 million—an unheard-of amount in 1940. The cost proved to be money well spent, however, as audiences, reviewers, and musicians all loved the film. "I can't think of a better way to have introduced the suspenseful story of that wizard and his young helper to a whole generation of listeners," says Gerald Lanning, a former Chicago music teacher. "One of my fondest memories of teaching was when a fourth grader came up to me after class and told me that she never knew that music could be that funny and that scary all at the same time."[39]

"Pinball Wizard"

The use of wizards has not been limited to classical music like *The Sorcerer's Apprentice.* Perhaps the best-known song that refers to a wizard is "Pinball Wizard," which appeared on the 1969 album *Tommy* by the Who, an English rock band. The group called their album a "rock opera," and the work tells the story of the title character, a young boy who has been the victim of violence and abuse. As a result of the trauma, Tommy becomes blind, deaf, and mute. Oddly enough, though, he also becomes amazingly skilled at the arcade game of pinball.

According to one verse of "Pinball Wizard," a competitor finds it nearly impossible to believe that someone with Tommy's disabilities can be such a wizard at a game that requires lightning fast reflexes and reactions:

> [He] ain't got no distractions
> Can't hear no buzzers and bells,
> Don't see no lights a flashing
> Plays by sense of smell.
> Always has a replay,
> Never seen him fail
> That deaf dumb and blind kid
> Sure plays a mean pin ball.[40]

Tommy was made into a movie in 1975. Members of the Who all starred in the film, including lead singer Roger Daltrey in the title role.

Wizards on the Tube

Television as well as film has provided audiences with memorable wizards. In the mid-1980s actor David Rappoport starred in *The Wizard*, a television series about an inventor named Simon who loses interest in developing new weaponry for the government and decides to devote himself to making amazing toys instead. His fascinating toys need interaction with the user to reach their full potential, and they range from special helicopters with hands-free remote controls to a stringless Yo-Yo and an assortment of voice-recognition mechanical animals such as owls, bears, and even guide dogs.

A more recent wizardly television series is *The Wizards of Waverly Place*, which ran for four seasons on the Disney Channel from October 2007 to January 2012. In it, the Russo family consists of a wizard father, Jerry, and a mortal mother, Theresa, along with their three teenage children, who are all wizards, too—at least for the time being.

The premise of the show is that only one person in each generation of the family is allowed to retain magical powers. After the children's training is complete, there will be a competition among them; the winner will remain a wizard, but the others will lose their magical abilities and become mortal.

Because his children's future is unknown, Jerry trains them to practice magic but not be dependent on it. He gives them magic lessons in a hidden wizard lair that can be accessed from their apartment or from the freezer in the family's sub shop. At all times, the family must keep their magical powers secret from their friends and neighbors.

Harry Potter

Although many wizards, including the Russos, have appeared in music, movies, and television, the undisputed wizard-king of pop

> # Did You Know?
>
> *Mr. Wizard*, a science-based television show for children, ran from 1954 to 1965 and was cited by the National Science Foundation for increasing youth interest in science. The show spawned fifty thousand school science clubs.

culture is Harry Potter, hero of J.K. Rowling's seven-book series and the films based on it. Harry, an eleven-year-old orphan living with relatives who dislike him, learns in the first book of the series, *Harry Potter and the Sorcerer's Stone,* that he is actually a wizard. Though the news is difficult for him to absorb, this revelation does explain some of the odd things that have happened to him, such as the shocking ability to communicate with a boa constrictor in the London Zoo's reptile exhibit.

Harry is invited to study magic at a special school, Hogwarts School of Witchcraft and Wizardry. There he finds that wizards and witches (in Rowling's books, witches are female wizards) reside in the same world as nonmagical humans known as Muggles. However, the magical population is largely able to hide its activities from the Muggles. For example, although Hogwarts is an enormous, beautifully landscaped castle, a special Muggle-repelling charm makes it look like nothing more than "a decrepit ruin with a sign saying 'Keep Out!'"[41]

Modeled After Merlin

The headmaster of Hogwarts is Albus Dumbledore, a wise and kindly man, whom Rowling has said she modeled after the character of Merlin in T.H. White's *The Once and Future King.* In fact, readers learn that Dumbledore has won the Order of Merlin medal—an award that benevolent wizards consider the most prestigious honor of all. According to the Rowling books, the Order of Merlin was actually founded by Merlin many centuries ago with the goal of promoting goodwill between wizards and Muggles.

Like White's Merlin, Dumbledore is eccentric. He loves to bowl and knit, and he is always interested in collecting new knitting patterns. When asked to name his greatest accomplishment, he admits that it was being featured on a Famous Wizards Chocolate Frog card. His odd sense of humor is evident when he speaks at the fall banquet to welcome new and returning Hogwarts students in *Harry Potter and the Sorcerer's Stone*:

> Albus Dumbledore had gotten to his feet. He was beaming at the students, his arms opened wide, as if nothing could have pleased him more than to see all of them there.

"Welcome!" he said. "Welcome to a new year at Hogwarts! Before we begin our banquet, I would like to say a few words. And here they are: Nitwit! Blubber! Oddment! Tweak!

"Thank you!"

He sat back down. Everybody clapped and cheered. Harry didn't know whether to laugh or not.[42]

Sharing the Wizarding Experience

Some of pop culture's most exciting wizardry is derived from Harry's school experiences. Besides spawning eight movies (the final book was made into two separate movies), Rowling's books have been so

The engaging world of wizards and witches comes to life in J.K. Rowling's popular Harry Potter books. The character Dumbledore (at far right in a scene from the 2005 movie Harry Potter and the Goblet of Fire) *is both wise and kind but does not hesitate to use his extraordinary powers when needed.*

popular that a theme park based on them was created: the Wizarding World of Harry Potter at Universal Studios in Orlando, Florida. Many of the park's visitors freely admit that they are delighted to have a way of experiencing the atmosphere of Hogwarts.

"It's phenomenal," says Derrick Snyder, a twenty-year-old New Yorker who has visited the Orlando park twice since it opened in 2010.

> This is a magic place. I grew up on these books and movies, and always, in the back of my mind, there was a piece of me that desperately wished I could be a wizard, too—kind of like how my dad says he wanted to be a cowboy when he was ten, because of watching Roy Rogers and the Lone Ranger. So that's my secret—I am a wizard wannabe, deep in my heart.[43]

Snyder insists that even as a twenty-year–old college student, he still wishes that Rowling's world, re-created in the theme park, were real:

> I'm not ashamed to admit it—the whole idea of camaraderie, the fun of hanging with a bunch of people who believe in the things you do, and having classes that teach you magic— I mean, what could be better? Who can honestly say they wouldn't want that? To fight for what is right and fair, against other wizards who aren't? If I'd had the chance, I would have jumped at it as a kid. That's why I came [to the Wizarding World of Harry Potter]. It's the closest I could get to living the dream I had then, and maybe still do. And yes, I bought a wand![44]

Virtual Wizarding

Whereas the Wizarding World of Harry Potter allows fans to get a close-up glimpse of the atmosphere in which Harry and his fellow students live, another wildly popular way in which wizard aficionados are experiencing a Hogwarts education exists online. Called Pottermore, the website was developed by J.K. Rowling and a team of artists and computer engineers. Pottermore opened its beta (test) version in 2011 to a limited number of users and decided to delay the grand opening to the public to work out glitches that could occur when millions of users logged onto the site. Pottermore finally opened in mid-April 2012.

"Many more Potter fans old and new will now be able to explore, discover and share the stories in a completely new way," the site's press release promises. "At Pottermore.com, they will be able to join Hogwarts School of Witchcraft and Wizardry, get sorted into one of the four houses, and have a wand choose them, before starting a journey through the storylines of these extraordinary books and discovering exclusive new writing from J.K. Rowling."[45]

Pottermore fan Jenni Miller-Kreiss says that being a wizard— even though merely a virtual one—is the most exciting thing she has ever done. "My cousin and I both are Potterheads," she laughs good-naturedly. "We've been wanting to do this since the site was first announced. Neither of us made it to the beta site, but we're on Pottermore now and it's awesome. I'm looking forward to all of it—especially dueling with other wizards."[46]

Miller-Kreiss says her parents have demanded a promise that she will limit her time on the website so that her real-life schoolwork does not suffer. "I get it," she says. "[My math teacher] Mr. Cartwright, would not be amused if my excuse for doing bad in algebra was that I was learning potions online, right?"[47]

Quidditch for All

Wizard sports are also making the crossover from literature to pop culture. For Harry Potter, one of the most enjoyable aspects of life at Hogwarts is the game of Quidditch, a sort of three-dimensional soccer played by teams of wizards flying on broomsticks. Fans of the books and movies have wondered how Quidditch could be adapted to be Muggle-friendly; students at Middlebury College in Vermont solved the problem of how to play the game even without flying broomsticks. Teams play on a field the size of a hockey rink, and players must hold a broomstick between their legs as they pursue the balls.

The golden snitch, a magical golden ball with wings that flies around on its own in the books, is part of Muggle Quidditch, too. However, in the Muggle version it consists of a tennis ball stuffed into a sock, carried by a cross-country runner dressed all in bright yellow or gold and sometimes wearing wings. When the runner is released along the sidelines, players from both teams may try to capture the snitch for a quick thirty points.

"I always loved the Quidditch aspect [of Harry Potter] and really wanted someone to turn it into an awesome video game," says Alicia Radford, a student at the University of Washington, "but when I heard about Muggle Quidditch at Middlebury, I was enchanted. Here were people taking a fictional sport that I loved and bringing it to life."[48]

Millions of people have eagerly embraced wizardry—through books, role-playing games, Quidditch tournaments, online wizard sites, and more. With so many opportunities to enter into the world of wizards—both ancient and modern—wizards are likely to remain a solid feature of popular culture.

Chapter 4

Evidence of Wizards

Many creatures and beings in legends and folklore—such as giants, trolls, and vampires—seem more the stuff of fantasy than reality. To many people, though, wizards seem not quite as improbable. Without question, societies all over the world have had their versions of wizards. They believed that some of their members had magical powers that ordinary humans did not. Today, some wonder whether wizards could have been, and perhaps are even today, real. Or are wizards simply fictitious characters who appeared in exciting stories from less enlightened times?

The First Wizards

A look back in time finds evidence of wizards—or at least people who were thought to have the powers associated with wizards. In many ancient cultures, a few special people—called shamans—seemed to possess unusual powers. They called on those powers to heal the sick and injured and to communicate with the spirits of the dead. They created potions, performed spells, and were even believed to be capable of transforming into animals. They often had special knowledge of plants and heightened awareness of natural events such as the changing seasons and patterns of the sun, moon, and stars.

Shamans used a variety of ways to put themselves into a special frame of mind for performing magic or communicating with the dead. Some shamans did special dances, and others used dreaming as a way to contact spirits. Some used plants with psychedelic properties to put themselves in a trance so they could more easily move across the boundary between the physical and spirit worlds.

The most celebrated physical evidence of ancient shamanism is a painting on the wall of a cave in rural France, not far from the Spanish border. Known as the Cave of the Three Brothers after the three young men who discovered it on their family's property in 1912, it is believed to have been home to prehistoric people about thirteen thousand years ago. Deep inside one part of the cave, the walls are decorated with a number of paintings depicting animals such as cattle, bison, and deer. One of these paintings, however, stands out among the rest. It is a thirteen-inch-tall (33cm) image of what appears to be a shaman—transformed into the form of a stag standing on its hind legs—performing a mysterious ritual, most likely one that will ensure good hunting for the tribe. It has become one of the most well known cave paintings in the world because it is the oldest and most vivid illustration of the importance of the shaman to prehistoric people.

Did You Know?

John Dee's wizardly prediction for a good day for Elizabeth I's coronation was January 15, 1559.

The Druids

Shamans and other wizards were important not only in prehistoric societies but also to societies that existed after the invention of writing. Some of the earliest wizards mentioned in written histories are the Druids, who lived in western Europe during what is known as the Iron Age. The Druids were the priests of the Celts, an early people who first settled in Britain in about 2000 BC. The Celts believed that the Druids were the intermediaries between the natural and spirit worlds.

The Druids' name comes from the words *drui*, meaning "oak tree," and *wyd*, the word for "knower" or "one who understands." Oak trees, and the acorns they produce, were thought to be sacred

The ancient Celts believed the Druids were intermediaries between the natural and spirit worlds. In one ritual, depicted by this painting from the late 1800s, Druid priests and priestesses dressed in ceremonial white robes use a golden scythe to cut sacred mistletoe from a tree.

to the Celtic gods, and a person who could understand the secret knowledge of those gods would be very powerful indeed. The Celts also considered mistletoe sacred, for it grows in the limbs of oaks and other tall trees. According to the first-century AD Roman historian Pliny, Druids cut down mistletoe with specially made golden scythes. They often made charms or necklaces from the mistletoe they harvested.

The Druids were believed to be capable of foreseeing events and were the guardians of the most dark, mysterious secrets of the universe. Not surprisingly, the Druids were very powerful, and even kings and military leaders deferred to them, notes wizard historian Robert Curran:

They interpreted the will of the Celtic gods and spirits with whom they were familiar, and no king or local ruler could afford to anger them, for while they were healers who saw the future and could encourage crops to grow and cause enemy's crops to die, they could also devastate a land with plague and bring famine and destruction at will.[49]

Mysterious Mist Makers

Julius Caesar, the greatest of the Roman generals, provided the first written eyewitness description of the Druids in the sixth book of his work called *Gallic Wars*. Caesar, who led his armies against the Celts during the first century BC, wrote that the Druids were believed to be the intermediaries between the Celts and the gods, and they were treated with respect and reverence:

The Druids preside in matters of religion . . . and interpret the will of the gods. They have the direction and education of youth. . . . The Druids never go to war, are exempted from taxes and military service. . . . They teach likewise many things relating to the stars and their motions, the magnitude of the world and our earth, the nature of things and the power and prerogatives of the immortal gods.[50]

Caesar noted that, in addition to providing knowledge about matters of nature, the Druids aided the Celtic army in ways that no Roman priests could have assisted Caesar's soldiers. Somehow the Druids were able to create thick, smoky mists at will on the battlefields, making it all but impossible for an opposing army to see and

A Shaman of Brazil

Ipupiara Mkunaiman is a shaman who was born into a remote Brazilian tribe. When he was young his mother urged him to attend the university, where he could best learn how to help his own and other indigenous peoples. During his final year there he became seriously ill, and doctors in the city were unable to help him.

His mother urged him to see the local shaman in their village, but Mkunaiman scoffed at the idea, insisting that if modern-day doctors could not help, surely a shaman could not either. Eventually, when it looked as though he were dying, Mkunaiman changed his mind and visited the shaman.

"When I saw the old man dancing and chanting around me, I said to myself, 'Ipupiara, you are done for,'" Mkunaiman recalls. "The old man opened up my mouth and poured a bowl of bitter, greenish stuff down my throat. I felt a warmth going through my body, and then I fell asleep. When I woke up, I was hungry. In one week I was walking and talking."

After that, Mkunaiman dedicated himself to studying shamanism and has learned the healing tradition of his people. Today he and his wife, who is also a healer, travel the country and give workshops teaching the wisdom of indigenous peoples.

Quoted in Hillary S. Webb, *Traveling Between the Worlds: Conversations with Contemporary Shamans.* Charlottesville, VA: Hampton Roads, 2004, p. 87.

target the Celtic warriors. According to historian Ronald Hutton, Druids were believed to be so powerful that they could stop a battle simply by stepping between the two armies.

A Real Merlin?

Like the Druids, the wizard Merlin appears not only in ancient legends but also in histories about the early days of Britain, leading some modern historians to believe that he may have been a real person—or perhaps two. These historians theorize that Geoffrey of Monmouth, who mentions Merlin in his 1136 work, *History of the Kings of Britain*, may have combined the stories of two people to create the composite character of Merlin.

One of these might have been a Welshman named Myrddin Wyllt, or Merlin the Wild. Myrddin Wyllt is said to have fled civilization to live alone in the woods after witnessing his two brothers being killed in battle. He felt comfortable only in the company of woodland creatures, and eventually he befriended the most ancient gods—who were worshipped long before the advent of Christianity. With their help, say some legends, he acquired the gift of prophecy.

The other possibility was Ambrosius Aurelianus, the youth named in the original story about King Vortigern trying to erect a tower. (Geoffrey of Monmouth later changed the name from Ambrosius Aurelianus to Merlin.) Says Curran:

> It's possible, of course, that Merlin didn't really exist, at least in the way we think about him. It's quite probable that he wasn't a single man at all but was created from stories about a combination of men who were extremely wise or who were believed to be great magicians. . . . Gradually these stories have all been drawn together and their heroes have become a single figure.[51]

> **Did You Know?**
>
> Though the title for the first Harry Potter book was *Harry Potter and the Philosopher's Stone*, the American publisher changed it to *Harry Potter and the Sorcerer's Stone*, believing American children would find the term *Philosopher* dull.

A New Definition of *Wizard*?

Many historians who investigate whether wizards like Merlin really existed believe that it might be necessary to redefine the word *wizard*. These historians suggest that wizards were not magicians but instead gifted and intelligent people who were far ahead of their time scientifically, technologically, and creatively.

For example, beginning in 1835 archaeologists found several golden cone-shaped objects in locations known as Bronze Age sites—meaning that the sites have been scientifically dated as being used as far back as 1500 BC. But although the uses of many archaeological finds, such as tools or weapons, were obvious, the purpose for these objects was not. The closest guess scientists had was that the artifacts were large vases.

In 2002, however, historians at Berlin's Museum for Pre- and Early History announced that they were confident that these objects were not vases but rather ceremonial hats worn by Bronze Age wizards. After carefully cleaning and studying the objects, they discovered that one of them was covered in 1,739 sun and half-moon symbols. Even more intriguing, those symbols made up a code invented by the fifth-century BC Greek mathematician Meton, believed to be the first to calculate the exact movements of the sun and moon. However, the mathematical formulas on the hat predate Meton's calculations by at least five hundred years.

Museum director Wilfried Menghin says that such a discovery forces archaeologists to rethink their view of those ancient people. Instead of being the most primitive of farmers with the most rudimentary tools, these farmers had wizards who were evidently able to take the guesswork out of deciding the best time to plant various crops. "The symbols on the hat are a logarithmic table which enables the movements of the sun and the moon to be calculated in advance," explains Menghin. "They suggest that Bronze Age man would have been able to make long-term, empirical astrological observations."[52]

John Dee

Another example of someone far ahead of his time was John Dee. Though believed by some to be the most skilled wizard of the sixteenth century, today his magic would be more likely explained by his ability to understand mathematics and astrology—considered wizardly arts in those days. Notes science author Roger Highfield, "The differences among astronomy, astrology, alchemy [the idea that it was possible to change base metals into gold], and magic were indistinct."[53]

Especially fascinating to Dee was the study of the stars and planets as well as the prediction of events based on their movement and position in the heavens. He became so famous for his accurate predictions that he was invited by several European rulers to work for them, but he chose to remain in his native England. There he served as court astrologer to Queen Elizabeth I; like most people of the time, she was a firm believer in the power of magic—both benevolent and wicked. In fact, after her predecessor, Queen Mary I, died in November 1558, Elizabeth asked Dee to consult the stars and planets and to suggest a day that would be luckiest for her own coronation, marking her accession to the throne.

Comets and Pig Bristles

Queen Elizabeth also consulted Dee about unusual or troubling occurrences. For example, when three wax voodoo-like figures were discovered in Windsor in 1578, Elizabeth was horrified to learn that one of them had been labeled "Elizabeth" on its forehead and was punctured with sharp pig bristles. The queen was sure the figure was evidence that someone was using Dark Arts against her.

Dee was summoned to the castle to calm the queen's fears, though there is no record of precisely how he did so. He did write in his journal that after the queen's council called upon him "to prevent the mischiefe," he obeyed the request with precautions taken "in godly and artificiall manner."[54] Dee insisted upon the latter, for he did not want to be thought of as someone who engaged in necromancy—even though he had done so in his youth. He demanded the presence of a man named Secretary Wilson throughout his proceedings as a witness who could verify that only appropriate magic was used.

On another occasion the year before, Dee had used his knowledge of astronomy to reassure the queen when a large comet appeared in

the sky. In those days the appearance of a comet was the cause of great fear among commoners and was considered to be especially bad luck should a king or queen view it, lest the realm be thrown into chaos. But after consulting with Dee for several days, Elizabeth confidently strode to the window one evening to catch a glimpse of the comet. Her horrified advisers begged her not to, but afterward, say historians, her display of bravery greatly enhanced her prestige.

Things to Consult in Divination

The following are just a few of the scores of divination terms for things wizards have studied in hopes of foretelling the future, according to Tom Ogden's *Wizards and Sorcerers: From Abacadabra to Zoroaster:*

alomancy—salt

apanthomancy—random contact with animals, including black cats

axiomancy—the vibration felt when using a hatchet

catoptromancy—moonlight reflected on a smooth surface

chiromancy—the palm of the hand

chromniomancy—onion sprouts

dendromancy—mistletoe

graphology—handwriting

oomantia—eggs

spodomancy—soot from a fireplace

tiromancy—cheese

xylomancy—pieces of wood by shape or size

The Alchemists and the Philosopher's Stone

Besides necromancy, another aspect of what was once considered wizardry is alchemy, an ancient form of chemistry. Alchemy was founded on the idea that it is chemically possible to turn base metals, such as lead, into gold. The key ingredient was something known as the philosopher's stone. Even a tiny bit of the stone, in any form, could be mixed with other common chemicals to turn the cheapest metal into the purest gold. Even more exciting, the stone could also grant immortality. The hitch, of course, was how to manufacture the philosopher's stone because the formula for it was shrouded in centuries of mystery.

Not surprisingly, the search for the elusive philosopher's stone was an irresistible lure for alchemists. Several claim to have discovered it, although Nicolas Flamel, a French bookseller who devoted every moment of his spare time to experiments in alchemy that might produce the philosopher's stone, is the most likely to have actually done so. Flamel supposedly died in 1418, but for centuries afterward people reported seeing him and his wife—once in 1776 at a Paris theater, and once in London during World War I.

Wizards Among Us

Although historical examples of wizards like Flamel abound, numerous self-described practitioners of various forms of magic and sorcery exist in the world today as well. Many people claim to have abilities that others do not—and as result, those without such abilities eagerly seek them out for advice. Whether they call themselves wizards, shamans, sorcerers, or fortune-tellers, they are widely believed to be able to tap into forces that others cannot access.

Scrying is one of the abilities that often sets wizards apart from others. Alexandra Chauran, a second-generation scryer, has been doing readings since she was a teenager. She says that the use of crystals can be very productive for some people— assisting them in planning for their future or in making important decisions. Although Chauran did not intend to become a scryer, there were signs even when she was a young girl that she had unusual powers:

> # Did You Know?
> The character of Nicolas Flamel in *Harry Potter and the Philosopher's Stone* was based on a real person who lived in France and practiced alchemy during the late 1300s and early 1400s.

The first time this happened was when I awoke from a terrible dream, sat bolt upright in my bed, and watched a candle on my dresser appear to light itself. I got out of bed and extinguished it, assuming that the wick had simply been smouldering since I had lit the candle a few hours previously. My sleepy destruction didn't stop at candles. Once, as I slept in my dorm room, my roommate watched me twitching comically from a bad dream, and then as I awoke, she witnessed the water glass by my bed explode in a shower of glass that fell in a circle everywhere but on my own body. She was fairly disturbed by this and chose to move out.[55]

Successful Scrying

When Chauran confided in her mother about the strange things that had happened to her, she was relieved to learn that her mother, too, had experienced odd things when she was a teenager. From that point on, Chauran began learning to channel the supernatural energy and use it for divination, or predicting the future. She soon acquired a crystal ball and learned how to use it.

Today, Chauran says, sometimes the things she sees during a reading are vague, but at other times they are quite clear. She gives the example of a client who called her because she had lost her two dogs, Sadie and Mollie. The woman was desperate to learn whether Chauran could tell her if the dogs were still alive and safe.

"Gazing into the crystal ball," Chauran writes, "I saw one of the dogs immediately, and I described a mutt who seemed to have some Labrador in her. The client confirmed that this was Mollie, just as I saw Mollie and the other dog running up a driveway that curved to the left with a blue truck and a dilapidated steel shed."[56]

Chauran told the client that the dogs were safe and tried to discover a clue as to where they were. She continues:

> I began to spell out some letters and numbers that began coming to me from the crystal ball, but they were jumbled. There was an S and then the number 4, and as I named some more letters, my client was able to unscramble them to a street name. She took her truck down the road to the street in question and found a house number that had those numbers, hearing her dogs barking from that house's backyard![57]

Alchemists, who were also once viewed as wizards, sought ways of turning lead and other metals into gold. In The Alchemist, *nineteenth-century painter William F. Douglas portrays an alchemist at work.*

Who Are the Wizards?

The experiences of Chauran and others like her demonstrate how the concept of wizardry has changed over the centuries. In the twenty-first century, technology and science have removed much of the day-to-day mystery early peoples confronted. Still, however, humans continue to experience powerful occurrences that defy rational explanation.

Anthropologist Susan Greenwood, doing research on magic, tells about one such occurrence that happened to Richard Mabey, a British naturalist and television producer, on a May night in Suffolk, England. To this day, Mabey says that he cannot explain exactly what occurred, other than recalling that he felt certain that the singing nightingale he was listening to was not really a bird at all:

> The setting was narcotic. A full moon, mounds of cow parsley glowing like suspended balls of mist, the fen [watery lowland] arching like a lustrous whaleback across the whole span of the southern horizon. The nightingale was a shaman, experienced, rhetorical, insistent. I sank into its charms, a willing initiate. A shooting star arced over the bush in which it was singing. As I edged closer, its song seemed to become solid, to be doing odd things to the light. I was aware that my peripheral vision was closing down, and that I had no sense of where I was in space. And then, for just a few seconds, the bird was in my head and it was me that was singing.[58]

According to Greenwood, Mabey insists that he does not believe in magic or the supernatural. That said, however, he has no other way to explain what happened to him that night.

Did Mabey encounter a wizard? Perhaps. If wizards still exist in the world today, they are unlikely to be the bearded, robed sorcerers of legends and folklore from generations ago. Twenty-first-century wizards may be geniuses and forward thinkers whose ideas about subjects ranging from technology to curing the most debilitating diseases may seem laughably impossible now but could, years in the future, become commonplace solutions. It is entirely possible, too, that wizards of today may include the shaman singing at twilight as a nightingale or the friendly young woman who may well be capable of seeing the future in her crystal ball.

Source Notes

Introduction: Dangerous Magic

1. D.L. Ashliman, ed., "The Black School," Folklore and Mythology Electronic Texts. www.pitt.edu.
2. Michael Hague, *The Book of Wizards*. New York: HarperCollins, 2008, p. 98.

Chapter One: Wizards of Wisdom in Literature and Lore

3. Robert Curran, *The Wizards' Handbook: An Essential Guide to Wizards, Sorcerers, and Magicians and Their Magic*. Hauppauge, NY: Barron's, 2011, p. 9.
4. J.K. Rowling, *Harry Potter and the Chamber of Secrets*. New York: Arthur A. Levine, pp. 216–17.
5. L. Frank Baum, "The Magic Bonbons," in *Magicians' Circle: More Spell-Binding Stories of Wizards and Wizardry*, ed. Peter Haining. London: Souvenir, 2003, p. 148.
6. Baum, "The Magic Bonbons," p. 148.
7. Baum, "The Magic Bonbons," p. 155.
8. Charles M. Skinner, *Myths and Legends of Our Own Land*, vol. 1. Philadelphia: J.B. Lippincott, 1896, p. 234.
9. Curran, *The Wizards' Handbook*, p. 69.
10. Quoted in Ruth Manning-Sanders, *A Book of Wizards*. New York: E.P. Dutton, 1967, p. 89.
11. Quoted in T.H. White, *The Once and Future King*. New York: Ace, 2011, p. 45.
12. White, *The Once and Future King*, p. 117.

Chapter Two: Wizards and the Dark Arts

13. Homer, *The Odyssey*. Bk. 10. http://classics.mit.edu.
14. Homer, *The Odyssey*.

15. Sigurd Towrie, "Finfolkaheem—the Ancestral Home," Orkney-jar. www.orkneyjar.com.

16. Deut. 18:10.

17. Richard Kieckhefer, *Forbidden Rites: A Necromancer's Manual of the Fifteenth Century.* University Park: Pennsylvania State University Press, 1997, p. 5.

18. La Vol, interview with author, April 3, 2012.

19. Quoted in Kieckhefer, *Forbidden Rites,* p. 96.

20. Quoted in Kieckhefer, *Forbidden Rites,* p. 96.

21. Quoted in Kieckhefer, *Forbidden Rites,* p. 96.

22. P.G. Maxwell-Stuart, *Wizards: A History.* Gloucestershire, UK: Tempus, 2004, p. 7.

23. Quoted in Maxwell-Stuart, *Wizards,* p. 7.

24. Quoted in Maxwell-Stuart, *Wizards,* p. 8.

25. Quoted in Maxwell-Stuart, *Wizards,* p. 8.

26. Quoted in Maxwell-Stuart, *Wizards,* p. 9.

27. Skinner, *Myths and Legends of Our Own Land,* pp. 94–95.

28. Quoted in S.E. Schlosser, *Spooky New York: Tales of Hauntings, Strange Happenings, and Other Local Lore.* Guilford, CT: Insiders' Guide, 2005, p. 111.

29. Schlosser, *Spooky New York,* p. 117.

30. Skinner, *Myths and Legends of Our Own Land,* p. 95.

31. Samuel Adams Drake, *A Book of New England Legends and Folklore in Prose and Poetry.* Boston: Roberts Brothers, 1884, p. 250.

32. Drake, *A Book of New England Legends and Folklore in Prose and Poetry,* p. 250.

Chapter Three: Wizards in Popular Culture

33. Stickboy Daily, "In Pictures: The Ten Best April Fools Stunts Ever." www.stickboydaily.com.

34. Quoted in Baseball Hall of Fame, "Ozzie Smith." http://baseballhall.org.

35. Ira Berkow, "To Cooperstown with Glove, the Wizard," *New York Times,* July 27, 2002. www.nytimes.com.

36. Quoted in Locke Peterseim, "Like Magic, Wizards' Name Becomes Cool," ESPN. http://espn.go.com.

37. Quoted in Dan Steinburg, "Why Abe Pollin Went from Bullets to Wizards," *Washington Post.* http://voices.washingtonpost.com.

38. Quoted in L. Frank Baum, *The Wonderful Wizard of Oz.* New York: HarperCollins, 1987, p. 189.

39. Gerald Lanning, interview with author, April 17, 2012.

40. Quoted in Metro Lyrics, "Pinball Wizard." www.metrolyrics.com.

41. Harry Potter Wiki, "Muggle-Repelling Charm." http://harry-potter.wikia.com.

42. J.K. Rowling, *Harry Potter and the Sorcerer's Stone.* New York: Scholastic, p. 123.

43. Derrick Snyder, interview with author, April 22, 2012.

44. Snyder, interview.

45. Quoted in Claire Armistead, "Pottermore Opens Its Doors for All, J.K. Rowling Announces," *Guardian,* April 14, 2012. www.guardian.co.uk.

46. Jenni Miller-Kreiss, interview with author, May 2, 2012.

47. Miller-Kreiss, interview.

48. Quoted in Jack McCluskey, "Forget the Movie . . . Try Quidditch," ESPN, July 22, 2009. http://sports.espn.go.com.

Chapter Four: Evidence of Wizards

49. Curran, *The Wizards' Handbook,* pp. 12–13.

50. Quoted in Tom Ogden, *Wizards and Socerers: From Abracadabra to Zoroaster.* New York: Checkmark, 1997, p. 58.

51. Curran, *The Wizards' Handbook,* p. 37.

52. Quoted in Tony Paterson, "Mysterious Gold Cones 'Hats of Ancient Wizards,'" *Telegraph,* March 17, 2002. www.telegraph.co.uk.

53. Roger Highfield, *The Science of Harry Potter.* New York: Viking, 2002, p. 218.

54. Quoted in John Dee Society, "Chapter VIII: Great Affairs, Celestial and Political." www.johndee.org.

55. Alexandra Chauran, *Crystal Ball Reading for Beginners: Easy Divination and Interpretation.* Woodbury, MN: Llewellyn, 2011, p. 65.

56. Chauran, *Crystal Ball Reading for Beginners,* p. 74.

57. Chauran, *Crystal Ball Reading for Beginners,* p. 74.

58. Quoted in Susan Greenwood, *The Anthropology of Magic.* New York: Berg, 2009, p. 6.

For Further Exploration

Books

Philip Carr-Gomm and Richard Heygate, *The Book of English Magic.* New York: Overlook, 2009.

Robert Curran, *The Wizards' Handbook: An Essential Guide to Wizards, Sorcerers, and Magicians and Their Magic.* Hauppauge, NY: Barron's, 2011.

Anita Dalal, *Native American Myths.* New York: Gareth Stevens, 2010.

Matt Dembick, ed., *Trickster: Native American Tales: A Graphic Collection.* Golden, CO: Fulcrum, 2010.

Arielle North Olson and Howard Schwartz, *More Bones: Scary Stories from Around the World.* New York: Puffin, 2009.

Beatrice Phillipotts, *The Wizard's Book of Spells.* Bath, UK: Palazzo, 2010.

Websites

Harry Potter Wiki (http://harrypotter.wikia.com/wiki/Main_Page). This is a database for all things Harry Potter. Fans of the books and movies can find information about the background of characters and plots as well as detailed explanations of spells, incantations, and potions.

Official Graham Phillips Website (www.grahamphillips.net). Created by British historian and author Graham Phillips, this site provides very helpful information about the Merlin of legend and history, using both art and text.

Orkneyjar: The Sorcerous Finfolk (www.orkneyjar.com/folklore/finfolk /index.html). This site includes background on the most interesting legends and background of the Finmen as well as the history, geography, and folklore of the Orkney Islands.

Pottermore (www.pottermore.com). Pottermore is an interactive site for Harry Potter fans to learn more about wizardry and the education that wizards receive in the books. Included is a great deal of backstory information written by J.K. Rowling especially for this website.

The Wizards of Waverly Place (http://tv.disney.go.com/disneychannel/wizardsofwaverlyplace/). This Disney Channel site contains information about the series, including plots, details about the actors, a virtual tour of their apartment and sub shop, as well as interactive games.

Index

Note: Boldface page numbers indicate illustrations.

Picture Credits

About the Author

Gail B. Stewart is the award-winning author of more than 250 books for teens and young adults. The mother of three grown sons, she lives with her husband in Minneapolis, Minnesota.